Getting into Government

Exploring

Checks and Balances

Barbara Krasner

Lerner Publications ◆ Minneapolis

Lerner Publications
An imprint of Lerner Publishing Group, Inc.
241 First Avenue North
Minneapolis, MN 55401 USA

For reading levels and more information, look up this title at www.lernerbooks.com.

Main body text set in Adrianna Regular.
Typeface provided by Chank.

Library of Congress Cataloging-in-Publication Data

Names: Krasner, Barbara, author.
Title: Exploring checks and balances / Barbara Krasner.
Description: Minneapolis : Lerner Publications, 2020. | Series: Searchlight Books. Getting into government | Includes bibliographical references and index. | Audience: Age 8–11. | Audience: Grade 4 to 6.
Identifiers: LCCN 2018059307 (print) | LCCN 2018060471 (ebook) | ISBN 9781541556751 (eb pdf) | ISBN 9781541555853 (lb : alk. paper) | ISBN 9781541574762 (pb : alk. paper)
Subjects: LCSH: Separation of powers—United States—Juvenile literature. | United States—Politics and government—Juvenile literature.
Classification: LCC JK305 (ebook) | LCC JK305 .K73 2020 (print) | DDC 320.473/04—dc23

LC record available at https://lccn.loc.gov/2018059307

Manufactured in the United States of America
1-46040-43363-5/2/2019

Contents

Chapter 1

CHECKS AND BALANCES . . . 4

Chapter 2

THE LEGISLATIVE BRANCH . . . 12

Chapter 3

THE JUDICIAL BRANCH . . . 19

Chapter 4

THE EXECUTIVE BRANCH . . . 24

Who's Right? • 29
Glossary • 30
Learn More about Checks and Balances • 31
Index • 32

CHECKS AND BALANCES

In 2005, the US Congress passed the Stolen Valor Act to punish people who lied about receiving high military honors. In 2012, the Supreme Court ruled that the Stolen Valor Act violated the right of free speech.

Then the office of the president stepped in. The president established an official list of people who have earned high military honors. In 2013, Congress revised and repassed the Stolen Valor Act.

President Barack Obama signs a bill into law in 2013.

Despite many political disputes, Speaker of the House Nancy Pelosi and President Trump share a handshake to show bipartisanship and willingness to cooperate.

Congress is part of the government's legislative branch. The Supreme Court makes up the judicial branch. The president represents the executive branch. The Stolen Valor Act is an example of how checks and balances work among the three branches of government.

The Three Branches

The country's founders wanted to create a system where the people hold the power. This is known as a democracy. They created a system of checks and balances to hold the government accountable to the people. Checks and balances would work to keep the different arms of government from acting alone.

George Washington (*top*), Thomas Jefferson, James Madison, and John Adams are among the founders of the United States.

Members of Congress gather together to hear the president's annual State of the Union address.

The legislative branch includes the House of Representatives and the Senate. These two groups make up Congress. Members of Congress are elected. The legislative branch is responsible for creating laws that best fit the interests of the people.

THE NINE SUPREME COURT JUSTICES COME FROM VASTLY DIFFERENT POLITICAL BACKGROUNDS.

Federal courts make up the judicial branch. Among them, the most powerful is the Supreme Court. The judicial branch is responsible for upholding the Constitution. The judicial branch decides court cases based on its interpretation of the Constitution.

President Donald Trump and Vice President Mike Pence display a newly signed bill.

The executive branch includes the offices of the president, vice president, and different federal departments. This branch carries out policies made by the legislative branch. The executive branch is responsible for enforcing the law.

Working Together

The different parts of government must work together for the checks and balances system to be effective. For example, the House and the Senate work together before sending a bill to the president for signing. If Congress can't agree on the terms of a bill, the bill may die before it reaches the executive branch.

Although consistently at odds, congressional leaders Nancy Pelosi and Lindsey Graham must be in communication and work together to move policies along.

Government Affects You

In 1990, the federal government spent 5 percent of its budget on programs for kids. This spending increased to more than 10 percent in 2010. In more recent years, the executive and legislative branches have been working together to shift the focus of federal funding. In 2017, the budget spent on kids dropped to 9.4 percent while funding for the military and elder care gradually increased. This was done to meet what these branches see as the nation's greatest needs.

Teachers and education advocates protest the budget cuts for education.

Chapter 2

THE LEGISLATIVE BRANCH

The legislative branch makes laws, but it also has other privileges that the executive and judicial branch do not have. For example, the legislative branch is the only arm with impeachment privileges. This means it can impeach, or charge with a crime, either the president or Supreme Court justices.

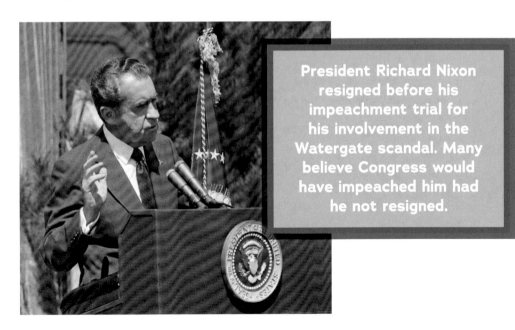

President Richard Nixon resigned before his impeachment trial for his involvement in the Watergate scandal. Many believe Congress would have impeached him had he not resigned.

Checking the Executive Branch

The executive branch has veto power. It can refuse to approve a bill proposed by Congress. However, Congress has the power to override the president's veto. This means a bill can pass even if the president vetoes it. But it can happen only if Congress holds a vote. Two-thirds of the House and the Senate must vote in favor of the bill for it to pass.

Among the various methods of voting in congress, a show of hands is usually used in small assemblies.

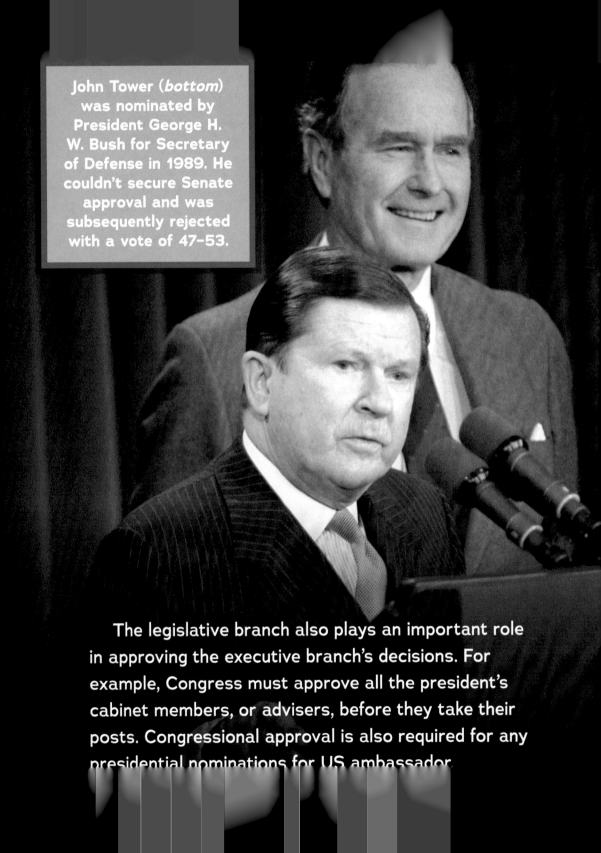

John Tower (*bottom*) was nominated by President George H. W. Bush for Secretary of Defense in 1989. He couldn't secure Senate approval and was subsequently rejected with a vote of 47–53.

The legislative branch also plays an important role in approving the executive branch's decisions. For example, Congress must approve all the president's cabinet members, or advisers, before they take their posts. Congressional approval is also required for any presidential nominations for US ambassador.

Congress decides whether to approve the president's federal budget proposal. While the president may offer suggestions on how to spend the federal budget, Congress makes the final decision.

Another way the legislative branch checks the executive branch is by being the only authority allowed to declare war even though the president is the commander in chief.

In order to declare war, an overwhelming majority of Congress must vote in favor of doing so. However, military force can be used without a formal declaration of war.

Checking the Judicial Branch

Congress has the right to change the number of justice seats in the Supreme Court. It also has the right to propose amendments, or changes, to the Constitution. Congress has the power to change or clarify laws that have been declared unconstitutional by the judicial branch too.

The Thirteenth Amendment was ratified in 1865 to abolish slavery in the United States.

Checking Itself

The House and the Senate check each other. Both sections of Congress must agree before a bill passes. If the House wants a bill passed and the Senate decides not to pass it, the bill does not pass. The House also has this power over the Senate.

Representative Bob Evans discusses a bill in the Mississippi House of Representatives.

That's a Fact!

In 1937, President Franklin Delano Roosevelt helped write a bill to increase the number of Supreme Court justices. He hoped his new Supreme Court nominations would rule in favor of parts of a program he'd proposed that had been denied. But Congress didn't pass the bill.

Roosevelt died during his fourth term in office. After Roosevelt's death, Congress passed the Twenty-Second Amendment. It limits the terms a president can serve to two.

Chapter 3

THE JUDICIAL BRANCH

Like the legislative branch, the judicial branch has functions that the other branches do not have. This branch checks the legislative branch by reviewing passed bills. It checks the executive branch too. For instance, the president can sign a bill into law and the judicial branch can declare it unconstitutional.

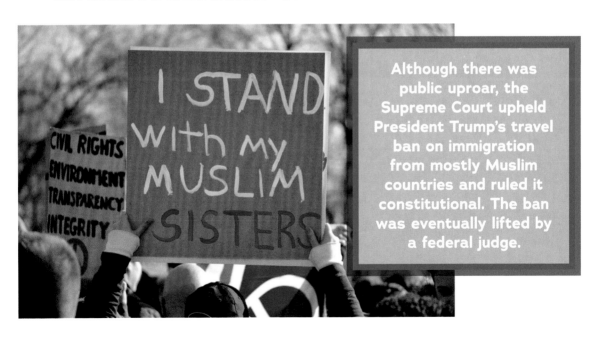

Although there was public uproar, the Supreme Court upheld President Trump's travel ban on immigration from mostly Muslim countries and ruled it constitutional. The ban was eventually lifted by a federal judge.

Justice Brett Kavanaugh was approved and sworn in as a Supreme Court justice.

Checking the Executive Branch

Although the president appoints Supreme Court justices, the president can't dismiss an appointed judge. Once a justice is appointed, the justice holds the seat for life or until retirement. If there's a presidential impeachment trial, the chief justice of the Supreme Court takes the place of the vice president as the head of the Senate to avoid a conflict of interest.

Checking the Legislative Branch

The judicial branch also checks the legislative branch during an impeachment of a president. It supervises the Senate in an impeachment trial. The judicial branch can also reverse laws passed by Congress with its power to rule laws unconstitutional.

Chief Justice William Rehnquist (*front*) is on his way to supervise the Senate during the impeachment trial of President Bill Clinton.

Checking Itself

The judicial branch checks itself. For example, the Supreme Court operates as one unit. Having an odd number of judge seats ensures no tie will occur. The Supreme Court can also overrule itself. It can reverse decisions it made previously.

The president and first lady pose with Justice Kavanaugh, his wife, and the Supreme Court justices during Justice Kavanaugh's confirmation.

Government Affects You

Early in his administration, President Donald Trump issued an executive order to prevent travel to and from seven mostly Muslim countries. He said he was protecting the United States from harm. In December 2017, a federal judge—a representative of the judicial branch—ruled to lift the ban. This allowed students from the seven countries to return to school in the United States. It also allowed families and friends to reunite.

Afnan Salem hopes to be reunited with her grandparents after Trump's ban is lifted.

Chapter 4

THE EXECUTIVE BRANCH

The executive branch deals with day-to-day living. This is why most government buildings feature a framed photo of the president on their walls. For instance, you may see the president's picture on the wall of your local post office or police department.

Presidential portraits are often framed and hung in government offices.

As commander in chief, the president is expected to address the troops and visit military bases.

Checking the Legislative Branch

One of the main ways the executive branch checks the legislative branch is through the president's ability to veto bills. The executive branch can dismiss a bill Congress has passed.

Only the president can call Congress to an emergency meeting. This occurs only when a big decision needs to be made quickly. The president serves as commander in chief of the army, navy, and other military services.

Checking the Judicial Branch

The executive branch checks the judicial branch through the selection of Supreme Court justices. When a seat opens up, the president nominates a candidate for confirmation by the Senate. Like the president's cabinet members, all presidential nominations need congressional approval.

As Trump's nomination for the Supreme Court, Nominee Kavanaugh was required to testify before the Senate Judiciary Committee.

After resigning from office, Nixon (*left*) transferred his presidential duties to Vice President Gerald Ford (*right*), who became president until the next election.

Checking Itself

Like the other branches, the executive branch checks itself. For instance, the vice president and the executive cabinet can decide whether the president is able to perform the presidential duties. If they find the president is not able to, the president would be removed from office and the vice president would become president.

That's a Fact!

The president has executive privilege. This means the president can choose not to share information with Congress or the courts. The privilege started with President George Washington. Still, the legislative and judicial branches can challenge a president's decision to withhold information.

President Dwight D. Eisenhower used his executive privilege forty-four times throughout his two terms.

Who's Right?

Those in favor of checks and balances argue that it maintains democracy. But some who question it believe the responsibilities of each branch of government overlap too much. They might say that it doesn't benefit a true democracy. They may even say it opens the country up to conflict over which branch should be doing what.

Do you think the checks and balances system is working? Why or why not?

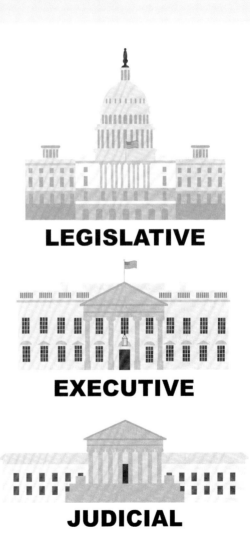

LEGISLATIVE

EXECUTIVE

JUDICIAL

Glossary

bill: a draft of a proposed law

budget: a yearly plan for how the US government will spend money

Congress: a group of elected officials who make laws. The US Congress is made up of the Senate and the House of Representatives.

Constitution: a set of principles that established the US government

democracy: a government system where the people hold the power

executive branch: the branch of government that enforces the law

federal: relating to the United States' national government

impeach: to charge a public official with a crime

judicial branch: the branch of government that upholds the Constitution

legislation: laws

legislative branch: the branch of government that creates the laws

override: to stop

Supreme Court: the highest and most powerful court in the US

unconstitutional: not consistent with the US Constitution

valor: an act of heroism and bravery

veto: to reject a bill

Learn More about Checks and Balances

Books

Buchanan, Shelly. *Our Government: Three Branches*. Huntington Beach, CA: Teacher Created Materials, 2015. Find out how the executive branch, legislative branch, and judicial branch work together to make justice for all possible.

Higgins, Nadia. *US Government through Infographics*. Minneapolis: Lerner Publications, 2015. Explore the government's three branches and the Constitution through fun graphics.

Richmond, Benjamin. *What Are the Three Branches of Government? And Other Questions about the U.S. Constitution*. New York: Sterling Children's Books, 2014. Get the answers to your questions about how the Constitution lays the foundation for the US government.

Websites

Ben's Guide to the US Government
https://bensguide.gpo.gov/
Explore the US government with an animated Ben Franklin as your guide.

Branches of the US Government
https://www.usa.gov/branches-of-government?source=kids
Get a view in infographics of the three branches of government and their duties.

Checks and Balances
https://www.factmonster.com/us/government-primer/checks-and-balances
Understand how the US government balances power between its three branches.

Index

bills, 4, 10, 13, 17–19, 25

Congress, 4–5, 7, 10, 12–18, 21, 25–26, 28

executive branch, 5, 9–15, 19–20, 24–27

federal budget, 11, 15

House of Representatives, 7, 10, 13, 17

impeachment, 12, 20–21

judicial branch, 5, 8, 12, 16, 19, 21–23, 26, 28

legislative branch, 5, 7, 9, 11–12, 14–15, 19, 21, 25, 28

Senate, 7, 10, 13–14, 17, 20–21, 26

Supreme Court, 4–5, 8, 12, 16, 18–20, 22, 26

Trump, Donald, 9, 19, 23, 24–25

vetoes, 13, 25

Photo Acknowledgments

Image credits: Lynch/MediaPunch Inc/Alamy Stock Photo, p. 4; ZUMA Press, Inc./Alamy Stock Photo, p. 5; World History Archive/Alamy Stock Photo, p. 6; White House Photo/Alamy Stock Photo, p. 7; dpa picture alliance/Alamy Stock Photo, p. 8; American Photo Archive/Alamy Stock Photo, p. 9; Gabriella Demczuk/Getty Images, p. 10; Jim West/Alamy Stock Photo, p. 11; Bettmann /Getty Images, pp. 12, 14; Bob Andres/Atlanta Journal-Constitution/Photographer, p. 13; New York Daily News/Getty Images, p. 15; Danita Delimont/Alamy Stock Photo, p. 16; Rogelio V. Solis /Photographer, p. 17; George Skadding/Getty Images, p. 18; Christopher Penler/Alamy Stock Photo, p. 19; Planetpix/Alamy Stock Photo, p. 20; David Hume Kennerly/Getty Images, p. 21; US Supreme Court/Alamy Stock Photo, p. 22; Martha Irvine/Photographer, p. 23; The Washington Post/Getty Images, p. 24; APFootage/Alamy Stock Photo, p. 25; Tom Williams-Pool/Getty Images, p. 26; Everett Collection Inc/Alamy Stock Photo, p. 27; Hank Walker/The LIFE Picture Collection/Getty Images, p. 28; JPL Designs/Shutterstock.com, p. 29.

Cover Images: Mark Wilson/Getty Images; photographer/Alamy Stock Photo.